STEP-BY-STEP

TAPAS & SPANISH
COOKERY

1996

Happy Birthday, Candy!
To a wonderful cook —
eat and be merry!
Love,
Christina

GREENWICH EDITIONS

Specially produced for Greenwich Editions
Unit 7, 202-208 New North Road
London, N1 7BJ

© Salamander Books Ltd., 1995

ISBN 0 862 880 211

Author: Hilaire Walden
Photographer: Jon Stewart

Printed and bound in Slovenia

OTHER TITLES IN THIS SERIES:

CONTENTS

INTRODUCTION

The Spanish cuisine is one of the most exciting, rewarding and varied in the world as it encompasses dishes that contain a kaleidescope of ingredients, prepared in myriad styles to suit perfectly every occasion, taste and diet. *Step-by-Step Tapas and Spanish Cookery* brings you the best examples of all these styles. There are simple dishes flavoured with herbs, vibrantly coloured and richly flavoured meat and poultry casseroles with equally tasty vegetable versions, as well as light, quickly cooked ones, and dishes based on rice and dried beans that are ideal one-pot meals, plus warming, hearty soups contrasted by those that are the epitome of summer eating.

There are all manner of fish recipes to serve for sophisticated eating or family suppers, with eggs for snacks and plenty of cakes and pastries to satisfy those with a sweet tooth.

The Spanish cuisine is essentially a family one, developing out of the ingenious exploitation of accessible local raw materials, and the imaginative and best use of foods that were readily available.

Based on simple ingredients, with its roots firmly in home cooking and pure country food, Spanish cooking is essentially hearty and unpretentious; ingredients are inexpensive, flavours direct, recipes easy and presentation straightforward with no unnecessary show. The criteria for the success of a dish is whether it tastes good.

In line with the trend that exists in respect to other national cuisines such as French and Italian, people, both Spaniards and foreigners, are now taking a closer look at 'traditional' Spanish food, increasing its reputation and expanding awareness of it. There is a growing band of 'new wave' chefs who are researching old dishes, refining them to suit modern tastes, and making Spanish food fashionable.

True, traditional Spanish cooking is many faceted. Indigenous foods and traditional culinary practices have been reinforced throughout the country's long history by the absorption of new ingredients and cultural influences from many different countries. The Romans left their imprint, principally in the irrigation of parts of the east coast, and the introduction of olives; while 700 years of Moorish occupation resulted in almonds, citrus fruits and fragrant spices becoming integral ingredients in Spanish cooking. The discovery of the New World resulted in the introduction, and wide acceptance of tomatoes, sweet and chilli peppers (capsicums), courgettes (zucchini), many types of beans, potatoes, chocolate and vanilla.

Furthermore, Spain covers areas as diverse as sparse mountain ranges, arid plains, fertile orchards and arable lands, olive and fruit groves, regions that are cold and wet, and those that are hot and dry, coasts facing two different seas – the Mediterranean and the Atlantic – and many rivers. Not surprisingly, each different area yields different foods and calls for a different type of cooking.

However, there are a number of ingredients and flavours that distinguish Spanish food. The olive is vital, particularly for its oil; Spain is the greatest consumer of olive oil in the world. Garlic is an indispensable element in the majority of dishes. Parsley is the popular herb, and nuts appear frequently, often ground to make a sauce. Onions, green and red peppers (capsicums) and tomatoes are the other constants.

FOOD OF THE REGIONS

The Basque province has both wonderful fish and seafood from the Atlantic ocean and some of the finest cattle, sheep and dairy foods in Spain. Portions are large, as is to be expected in a cold climate, but the cooking has a certain refinement. Dishes cooked *al chilindrón*, in a flavourful sauce based on the particularly good local red peppers (capsicums), and tomatoes, onions and garlic, are typical of Navarra and Aragon. Trout from the clear mountain streams that rise in the Pyrenees are a regional favourite, especially cooked with ham.

The food of Catalonia is exciting and richly varied and features interesting sauces, such as Romesco and Allioli (see page 34), aromatic herbs and noticeable similarities with French Mediterranean food, such as Zarzuela (see page 40), a close cousin of bouillabaise.

Valencia and Murcia form one of the most densely populated and richest agricultural areas of Europe, and exhibit distinct Moorish influences. Here there are groves of oranges and almonds, large market gardens and rice fields. The last two provide the ingredients for authentic Paella Valenciana – the addition of fish and shellfish is a modern adaptation that has become universally popular. Andulacía is the land of olives, olive oil and sizzling fried foods, particularly the varied sea and shellfish from around the long coastline. In contrast, Extremadura is a land of tough, hardy countrymen, and simple hearty cooking with many stew-type dishes.

The vast, exposed Central Plain produces Spain's most well-known cheese, Manchego (see page 9), as well as many other sheeps' milk cheeses. The area is most generally throught of as a land of roasts, principally young lamb and suckling pigs.

Galicia and Asturias are renowned for the quality of the fish and shellfish, and as the home of excellent Empanadas (see page 18). The climate is comparatively cold and wet, so appetities tend to be hearty and the local dishes correspondingly warming and filling. Locally produced cider is popular for drinking and also for using in cooking.

EATING PATTERNS

The traditional breakfast is usually eaten in cafés and consists of churros with large cups of hot chocolate in which the churros are dunked. Coffee and sweet cakes or a light snack are eaten at mid-morning. Lunch, the main meal of the day, is at 2 o'clock, but is often preceded by tapas, usually taken at a bar or café on the way home or to a restaurant. Work is returned to in the late afternoon. About 6 o'clock is the time for a *merienda*, light snack, with tapas being eaten from about 8 until 10 o'clock, when it is time for dinner. This is usually lighter than lunch.

TAPAS

Originally, and still in some bars today, tapas were simply a few olives or almonds, and perhaps a selection of cheeses, sausages and serrano ham and possibly cubes of tortilla served, often free, to accompany a glass of fino sherry. But nowadays, tapas have come to encompass more or less any hot or cold dish that can be served in small portions, and they may be quite substantial. They are displayed along the lenth of the counter of a bar or café to be ordered in a group, or individually.

Although quintessentially Spanish, tapas are so well-suited to today's style of casual eating, that they have caught the popular imagination outside Spain. A selection of tapas is ideal for an interesting informal meal, and they are wonderful fare for a party, buffet, picnic or barbecue. Most can be made quickly and easily, a great many can be made in advance and served at room temperature while others can be partly prepared and then finished at the last minute before serving.

INGREDIENTS

Cheese: Although Spain produces about 200 cheeses, only Manchego enjoys any degree of reknown, and is the only one exported in quantity. Manchego may be mild and quite soft, or strong and hard. It is made from sheeps milk, so is quite expensive. If Manchego is not available, use freshly cut Parmesan cheese.

Chillies: These play an important role in Spanish cooking, adding not only heat but distinct flavour to dishes. Different varieties of chillies impart different flavours and degree of heat. Generally, large chillies are milder than small ones, whilst dried ones are often hotter than fresh. Red chillies are ripened green chillies, and so they have a sweeter, more rounded flavour compared to the fresher, 'green' taste of the immature form. Avoid touching your eyes or any cuts, and always wash hands thoroughly afterwards. If you have sensitive skin, wear rubber gloves when handling chillies.

Chorizo: The best chorizo contains as much as 95% pork. Other ingredients are pork fat, salt, garlic and paprika, which gives it the pronounced red colour. The most widely known and available chorizos are fully cured and can be eaten without cooking, for example, as a tapas or in salads. There are two degrees of spiciness, picante (hot) and dulce (mild).

The other type of chorizo, which has to be cooked, is found in stews and in bean and potato dishes, which will be coloured red by the leeching out of the paprika in the chorizo. These chorizos are short and stubby and come linked together in the same way as English sausages. They sometimes have added flavour from being smoked over oak fires. Oregano is also sometimes added.

For the best and truest flavour use good Spanish chorizo, but if unavailable use paprika sausages, which are usually found in Italian delicatessens.

Garlic: This is essential in Spanish cooking. Use the freshest possible – if there is any sign of a green shoot in the centre of a clove, remove it as it imparts a bitter taste to a dish. Buy garlic bulbs that are plump and firm and store them in a cool, dry place. Raw garlic has a pungent flavour, but when it is cooked, the taste mellows to give a subtle background flavour, and whole cloves can be eaten. Chopping garlic gives a more pronounced flavour than crushing it.

Herbs: Parsley is an important herb in Spanish cooking. The flat-leaved, Continental type is used. Oregano makes an occasional appearance, while bay leaves and thyme are quite widely used, especially in dishes which require long cooking. The presence of mint, most popularly with broad beans and chicken, is a legacy left by the Moors. Fresh herbs give a better flavour then dried ones. However, if you do have to use dried herbs, reduce the amount in the recipes by a half to two thirds.

Ham: The most well known Spanish ham is *jamón serrano*. This is a raw, air dried ham and is often eaten in thin, though not wafer thin, slices carved along the grain as a tapa. The best *jamón serrano* comes from the black Iberian pig, but the supply is limited. *Jamón serrano* is also used for cooking, when it is more thickly sliced so it can be chopped into chunks. Italian prosciutto is the nearest substitute.

Olive oil: Olive oil lends a characteristic flavour to many dishes. For general cooking, use a pure Spanish olive oil as it has a mild flavour, and keep the more distinctly flavoured, and more expensive, virgin oils for dressings. Keep olive oil in a cool, dark place, but not the refrigerator, and use within a year.

Onions: Yellow Spanish onions have a sweet and mild taste.

Paprika: *Pimentón dulce*, produced from ground dried red peppers, is an essential element in Spanish cooking, adding a characteristic flavour and colour to many dishes. It is added at the beginning of the cooking and is fried to release its flavour. However, it should not be overheated otherwise it will taste burnt.

Peppers (capsicums): These come in progressive stages of ripening, from green through yellow to red, but red ones, being the ripest, are sweeter and more rounded in flavour.

To remove the skin from peppers, (capsicums), either grill halved peppers (capsicums) skinside uppermost, 5 cm (2 in) away from the grill for 8-10 minutes, or bake them in an oven preheated to 200C (400F/Gas 6) for 20-40 minutes until they are blistered and charred (this also adds a delicious smoky flavour), leave until cool enough to handle, then scrape or peel off the skin.

Thin-skinned, small, long and pointed piquillo peppers (capsicums) are the ones that are used for stuffing; they are sold in bottles, which are generally best, or in cans. If unavailable, substitute ordinary canned small red peppers (capsicums).

Dark red *ñora* peppers (capsicums) are sold dried and can be seen in Spain in strings hanging from windows or in markets or grocers. They do not have much flesh, but their flavour and colour is concentrated. To use them, pull out the stalk and shake out as many seeds as possible. Soak them in cold water for 30-60 minutes to soften the skin, then cut in half and scrape out the flesh using a teaspoon. Paprika pepper can be substituted for *ñoras*.

Rice: Spanish rice is medium-grained, similar to Italian arborio (risotto) rice, but whereas a risotto is stirred to encourage the rice grains to become sticky, the rice for a paella must be left undisturbed during cooking once the liquid has been added.

Saffron: Although expensive only a few threads are needed to give a wonderful flavour and aroma to a dish for four people. For the best flavour, use genuine Spanish saffron threads or strands, and avoid saffron powder as it may have added ingredients that give colour but no flavour. To gain maximum flavour from saffron, crush the threads with a small pestle and mortar or between two teaspoons, then soak in a little hot water.

Sherry vinegar: This is made from Spanish sherry, and is rich and concentrated, so very little is needed to enhance the flavour of a dish.

Tomatoes: Well-flavoured tomatoes are important to the success of many Spanish dishes. For the recipes in this book use irregular-shaped 'marmande' or beefsteak tomatoes, but avoid Dutch ones as they lack the flavour of those grown further south, under a hotter sun. To skin tomatoes, put them in a bowl, pour over boiling water, leave for about 30 seconds, then remove from the water one at a time and slip off the skin. It should come away easily.

EQUIPMENT

Pestle and mortar: This is used extensively, but the end of a rolling pin and a small bowl can be substituted for crushing spices and small amounts of ingredients, and a small blender or food processor for larger volumes.

Cazuelas: Cazuelas are earthenware casseroles that are unglazed outside and glazed inside. They are the most commonly used pieces of cooking equipment in Spain. *Cazuelas* are available in a wide variety of shapes, sizes and depths from fairly shallow small ones for individual portions of tapas, to deep ones used for poultry and meat casseroles. It is wise to use a heat diffuser when cooking on top of the stove as direct contact with heat can cause a *cazuela* to crack.

A *cazuela* should be seasoned before using it for the first time to avoid cracking: half fill with water and a generous splash of vinegar, bring gently to the boil, then boil until the liquid has evaporated. *Cazuela* rarely have lids but foil can be used for a covering.

Paella: Although a wide frying pan can be used for making paellas, a proper paella pan with a thick metal base and sloping sides is better.

STUFFED MUSSELS

1.5 kg (3 lb) large mussels in their shells
85 ml (3 fl oz/⅓ cup) dry white wine
85 ml (3 fl oz/⅓ cup) olive oil
25 g (1 oz/½ cup) fresh breadcrumbs
3 tablespoons finely chopped fresh parsley
1 tablespoon finely chopped fresh oregano
2 cloves garlic, finely crushed
pinch cayenne pepper
salt and freshly ground black pepper
1 large lemon, quartered
parsley sprigs and lemon slices, to garnish

Scrub mussels and remove beards. Discard any mussels that remain open when tapped firmly. Put in a large saucepan with wine.

Cover and boil for 4-5 minutes, shaking pan occasionally, until shells open. Strain and reserve liquid. Discard any shells that do not open. Discard top shells, leaving mussels on remaining shells. In a small bowl, stir together 3 tablespoons oil, the breadcrumbs, herbs, garlic, cayenne and salt and pepper. Moisten with a little of the reserved mussel cooking liquid, if mixture is dry.

Preheat grill. Divide breadcrumb mixture between mussels on their shells. Place on a baking tray. Sprinkle with remaining olive oil and place under hot grill for 1-2 minutes until topping is crisp and golden. Squeeze over plenty of lemon juice and serve garnished with parsley sprigs and lemon slices.

Serves 4-6.

SIZZLING PRAWNS

100 ml (3½ fl oz/scant ½ cup) olive oil
4 cloves garlic, finely crushed
1 small fresh red chilli, seeded and chopped
350 g (12 oz) raw prawns, peeled
sea salt
2 tablespoons chopped fresh parsley
lemon wedges and bread, to serve

Heat oil in 4 individual flameproof earthen-ware dishes over a high heat. Add garlic and chilli, cook for 1-2 minutes, then add prawns and sea salt.

Cook briskly for 2-3 minutes. Stir in parsley. Serve quickly so the prawns are sizzling in the oil, and accompany with lemon wedges and bread to mop up the juices.

Note: One large dish, or a frying pan, can be used instead of individual dishes.

Serves 4.

GRILLED PRAWNS

450 g (1 lb) raw Mediterranean (king) prawns, peeled,
leaving tail shells on
5 tablespoons extra virgin olive oil
½ clove garlic, finely crushed
juice 1 lemon
salt and freshly ground black pepper
1 small beefsteak tomato, peeled, seeded and finely
chopped
½ small, fresh red chilli, finely chopped
1 tablespoon finely chopped fresh parsley
parsley sprigs and lemon slices and rind, to garnish

Using a small sharp knife, make a fine cut
along spine of each prawn and remove black
vein. Thread prawns onto small skewers and
place in a shallow dish. In a small bowl, stir
together 2 tablespoons oil, the garlic, 1½
tablespoons lemon juice and salt and pepper.
Pour over prawns and leave for 30 minutes.

Preheat grill. Lift prawns from dish and place
on grill rack; brush with any liquid remaining
in dish and grill for 3-4 minutes until bright
pink. In another small bowl, stir together
remaining oil and lemon juice, the tomato,
chilli, parsley and salt and pepper. Spoon
over hot prawns and serve garnished with
parsley sprigs and lemon slices and rind.

Serves 4.

ROAST PEPPER SALAD

4 red peppers (capsicums), peeled, seeded and cut into
   strips
4 canned anchovy fillets, cut lengthways into slivers
1 tablespoon capers (optional)
1 tablespoon finely chopped fresh parsley
8 tablespoons virgin olive oil
salt and freshly ground black pepper

Place peppers (capsicums) in a shallow dish.
Arrange anchovy fillets on top and sprinkle
with capers, if using.

In a small bowl, beat together parsley, oil,
pepper and just a little salt, if liked. Trickle
the dressing over peppers (capsicums),
anchovies and capers.

Serves 4.

MARINATED SARDINES

450 g (1 lb) fresh sardines or anchovies, cleaned
sea salt and freshly ground black pepper
115 ml (4 fl oz/½ cup) white wine vinegar
1 clove garlic, finely crushed
2 tablespoons finely chopped Spanish onion
3 tablespoons olive oil
2 teaspoons lemon juice
diced peeled red pepper (capsicum) and chopped
    fresh parsley, to garnish

Place one fish skin-side uppermost on work surface and press thumbs firmly along backbone; turn fish over, pull out backbone from head and cut free at tail. Repeat with remaining fish.

Lay fish in a shallow, non-metallic dish. Sprinkle over sea salt, vinegar, garlic and onion. Cover and leave in a cool place overnight. Drain and rinse fish; reserve some of onion. Dry fish on absorbent kitchen paper, then place on a serving plate. In a small bowl, mix together oil, lemon juice, reserved onion and salt and pepper. Pour over fish and garnish with diced red pepper (capsicum) and parsley.

Serves 4.

CHEESE FRITTERS

olive oil for deep frying
2 egg whites
115 g (4 oz/1 cup) finely grated mature Manchego or
   Parmesan cheese
55 g (2 oz/1 cup) fresh breadcrumbs
about 1 tablespoon finely chopped fresh herbs, such as
   parsley, chives and thyme
salt, freshly ground black pepper and paprika
thyme sprigs, to garnish

Heat a deep fat fryer two thirds filled with
olive oil to 180C (350F).

Meanwhile, in a bowl, whisk egg whites until
stiff but not dry. Lightly fold in cheese, breadcrumbs and herbs. Season with salt, pepper
and paprika.

Form egg white mixture into small walnut-
size balls, adding balls to hot oil as they are
shaped. Fry for about 3 minutes until golden.
Transfer to absorbent kitchen paper to drain.
Serve hot, garnished with sprigs of thyme.

Serves 4.

EMPANADA

450 g (1 lb/4 cups) strong flour
salt
2 teaspoons easy-blend dried yeast
300 ml (10 fl oz/1¼ cups) tepid milk
2 egg yolks
dash anise
1 egg, beaten
FILLING:
2 tablespoons olive oil
2 Spanish onions, chopped
225 g (8 oz) beefsteak tomatoes
400 g (14 oz) can tuna in oil, drained
1 large red pepper (capsicum)
6 black olives, stoned and quartered
4 saffron threads

Sift flour and pinch of salt into a bowl. Stir in yeast. Stir milk into egg yolks, add anise, then slowly pour into flour, stirring constantly. Beat for 5-10 minutes until dough comes cleanly away from bowl.

Turn onto a lightly floured surface and knead until smooth and elastic. Form into 2 even-sized balls, place in an oiled bowl, cover and leave in a warm place until doubled in volume, about 1 hour.

To make filling, heat oil in a frying pan, add onions and cook, stirring occasionally, for about 4 minutes until softened. Peel, seed and chop tomatoes, stir into pan and simmer until thickened. Flake tuna. Peel and chop pepper (capsicum) and stir into pan with tuna and olives. Crush saffron threads and dissolve in 2 tablespoons hot water. Add to pan. Simmer until well combined, then set aside.

Preheat oven to 200C (400F/Gas 6). Grease a baking sheet. On a lightly floured surface, roll out each piece of dough to a thin rectangle or square. Transfer one piece to baking sheet.

Spread filling over dough, leaving a narrow border clear all the way round. Dampen border with water. Cover with the other piece of dough and press edges together. Glaze with beaten egg and cut a slit in centre. Bake for 15-20 minutes until golden. Serve warm, cut into rectangles or squares.

Serves 4-6.

SPICY OLIVES

450 g (1 lb) green or black olives
1 sprig oregano
1 sprig thyme
1 teaspoon finely chopped fresh rosemary
2 bay leaves
1 teaspoon fennel seeds, bruised
1 teaspoon finely crushed cumin seeds
1 fresh red chilli, seeded and chopped
4 cloves garlic, crushed
olive oil to cover

Using a small sharp knife, make a lengthways slit through to stone of each olive. Put olives into a bowl. Stir in oregano, thyme, rosemary, bay leaves, fennel seeds, cumin, chilli and garlic.

Pack olive mixture into a screw-top or preserving jar. Pour over sufficient oil to cover, close the lid and leave for at least 3 days, shaking jar occasionally, before using.

Serves 6.

SPICY PORK KEBABS

2 teaspoons paprika
1 teaspoon finely crushed coriander seeds
1½ teaspoons ground cumin
1 teaspoon finely chopped fresh oregano
¼ teaspoon ground ginger
large pinch each ground cinnamon, cayenne pepper and
    grated nutmeg
1 bay leaf, finely crumbled
2 tablespoons olive oil
salt and freshly ground black pepper
450 g (1 lb) boned loin of pork, cut into 2.5 cm
    (1 in) cubes
lemon slices and bay leaves, to garnish

In a bowl, mix together all ingredients, except pork and garnish. Add pork and stir to coat evenly with marinade. Cover bowl and leave in refrigerator for 8-12 hours, turning pork occasionally.

Preheat grill. Thread the pork onto small skewers. Cook under hot grill for about 7 minutes, turning occasionally, until pork is cooked through but still juicy. Garnish with lemon slices and bay leaves and serve hot.

Serves 4.

ANCHOVY-STUFFED MUSHROOMS

25 g (1 oz) fresh bread without crusts, crumbled
4 tablespoons milk
450 g (1 lb) medium cap mushrooms
115 g (4 oz) green (unsmoked) bacon, finely chopped
4 canned anchovy fillets, finely chopped
1 clove garlic, finely chopped
1 egg, beaten
3 tablespoons finely chopped fresh parsley
pinch chopped fresh oregano
salt and freshly ground black pepper
4 tablespoons dry breadcrumbs
4 tablespoons olive oil
oregano sprigs, to garnish

Preheat oven to 200C (400F/Gas 6). Oil a large baking tray. Put fresh bread in a small bowl, add milk and leave to soak. Remove stalks from mushrooms and chop finely. Put into a bowl with bacon, anchovy fillets, garlic, egg, parsley, oregano and salt and pepper. Squeeze soaked bread dry, add to bacon mixture and mix together well.

Divide bread mixture between open side of mushroom caps, piling mixture into small mounds. Place on baking tray and sprinkle with dry breadcrumbs. Trickle oil over mushrooms. Bake on top shelf of oven for 20-30 minutes until top of stuffing is crisp. Leave to stand for a few minutes before serving, garnished with oregano.

Serves 4-6.

— MUSHROOMS WITH GARLIC —

3 tablespoons olive oil
2 cloves garlic, finely chopped
450 g (1 lb) mushrooms, cut into large pieces
4 tablespoons fino sherry
55 g (2 oz) pine nuts
squeeze lemon juice
salt and freshly ground black pepper
2 tablespoons chopped fresh parsley

In a large frying pan, heat oil, add garlic and cook over a fairly high heat for about 3 minutes until just beginning to brown.

Stir mushrooms, sherry and pine nuts into pan and continue to cook until mushroom juices have almost evaporated. Add lemon juice and seasonings to taste, then stir in parsley and serve.

Serves 4.

POTATOES WITH ALLIOLI

450 g (1 lb) small potatoes, preferably new, unpeeled
sea salt
1 tablespoon finely chopped fresh parsley
ALLIOLI SAUCE:
6-9 cloves garlic
salt and freshly ground black pepper
about 150 ml (5 fl oz/²⁄₃ cup) olive oil

Add potatoes to a saucepan of boiling salted water and boil until tender.

Meanwhile, make sauce. Using a pestle and mortar, crush garlic with a little salt. Work in oil a drop at a time; as the sauce thickens the oil can be added more quickly. Season with salt and pepper.

Drain potatoes well. Immediately potatoes are cool enough to handle, cut into bite-size chunks and toss with sea salt and the allioli. Sprinkle with parsley and serve warm.

Serves 4-6.

Variation: Pound 1 egg yolk with the garlic, then add juice of ½ lemon to finished sauce.

PRAWN-STUFFED EGGS

4 hard-boiled eggs, peeled
4 tablespoons mayonnaise
55 g (2 oz) peeled prawns, chopped
salt, cayenne pepper and lemon juice, to taste
lettuce leaves, to serve
whole prawns, paprika and parsley sprigs, to garnish

Slice the eggs in half lengthways. Using a teaspoon, scoop the yolks into a small bowl; reserve the white shells.

Add the mayonnaise to the bowl and, using a fork, mash with the yolks and prawns. Add salt, cayenne pepper and lemon juice to taste.

Divide the prawn mixture between the egg whites. Arrange on lettuce leaves and garnish with whole prawns, paprika and parsley sprigs.

Serves 4.

TUNA CROQUETTES

440 g (15½ oz) can tuna in brine
about 200 ml (7 fl oz/scant 1 cup) milk
2 tablespoons olive oil, plus extra for deep frying
¼ Spanish onion, finely chopped
4 tablespoons plain flour
1½ tablespoons finely chopped fresh parsley
2 tablespoons lemon juice
3 eggs, beaten
salt and freshly ground black pepper
175 g (6 oz/3 cups) fresh breadcrumbs
lemon wedges and watercress, to serve

Drain tuna and make up juice to 350 ml (12 fl oz/1½ cups) with milk. Flake tuna; set aside.

Heat 1 tablespoon olive oil in a small saucepan, add onion and cook for about 4 minutes until soft but not coloured. Stir in flour and cook, stirring, for 2 minutes. Remove from heat and slowly stir in half the milk mixture. Return to heat and bring to boil, stirring in remaining milk mixture. Simmer for 8 minutes, stirring occasionally. Off the heat, stir in tuna, parsley, lemon juice, 1 egg and salt and pepper.

Pour into a shallow dish, cool, cover and refrigerate for 2-3 hours. Put remaining eggs and the breadcrumbs into separate bowls. Dip small balls of tuna mixture first in egg then breadcrumbs to coat evenly. Half fill a deep fat fryer with oil and heat to 180C (350F). Fry tuna balls in batches for 2-3 minutes until crisp and golden. Using a slotted spoon, transfer to absorbent kitchen paper to drain. Serve hot with lemon wedges and small sprigs of watercress.

Serves 4.

VEGETABLE SALAD

450 g (1 lb) potatoes, unpeeled
1 large carrot, peeled and halved or quartered
55 g (2 oz) peas
115 g (4 oz) green beans
2 tablespoons chopped Spanish onion
1 small red pepper (capsicum), peeled, seeded and
    chopped
4 small pickled gherkins, chopped
1½ tablespoons capers
8-12 black or anchovy-stuffed olives
150 ml (5 fl oz/⅔ cup) mayonnaise
1 hard-boiled egg, sliced
chopped fresh parsley, to garnish

Boil potatoes in their skins until tender. Cool, peel, then cut into dice. Boil carrot, peas and beans. Dice carrot and cut beans into short lengths.

Put potatoes, carrot, peas and beans into a bowl and stir in onion, pepper (capsicum), gherkins, capers, olives and mayonnaise while vegetables are still warm. Leave to cool. Arrange hard-boiled egg and chopped parsley on top before serving.

Serves 4.

HUEVOS FLAMENCA

2 tablespoons olive oil
½ Spanish onion, finely chopped
2 cloves garlic, crushed
4 slices serrano ham, chopped
1 small red pepper (capsicum), seeded and finely
  chopped
pinch paprika
1 large beefsteak tomato, peeled, seeded and chopped
85 g (3 oz/¾ cup) cooked fresh peas, or frozen peas
115 g (4 oz) cooked green beans
1 teaspoon tomato purée (paste), (optional)
salt and freshly ground black pepper
4 eggs
4 slices cooking chorizo
1 tablespoon chopped fresh parsley

Preheat oven to 230C (450F/Gas 8). In a frying pan, heat oil, add onion and garlic and cook for about 4 minutes, stirring occasionally, until softened but not browned. Add half the ham and the pepper (capsicum). Fry for 2 minutes, then stir in paprika. Heat for 1 minute. Add tomato. Simmer for about 10 minutes until reduced to a fairly thick purée. Add peas and beans, and a little tomato purée (paste) if necessary. Season.

Pour into a shallow ovenproof dish, or 4 individual dishes. Form 4 shallow depressions in mixture. Carefully break eggs into depressions, allowing whites to flow over surface. Scatter remaining ham over the top and lay a chorizo slice on yolks. Bake for 8-10 minutes until egg whites are just set and yolks still moist, or for about 15 minutes if firmer eggs are preferred. Sprinkle with parsley and serve.

Serves 4.

— TORTILLA WITH RED PEPPER —

6 tablespoons olive oil
450 g (1 lb) potatoes, diced
1 Spanish onion, chopped
1 red pepper (capsicum), seeded and chopped
5 eggs
1 tablespoon chopped fresh parsley
salt and freshly ground black pepper

Heat oil in a large, heavy frying pan, prefer-ably non-stick. Add potatoes, onion and red pepper (capsicum) to pan. Cover and cook over a low heat for 15-20 minutes until soft but not brown, stirring occasionally to prevent sticking.

Drain off and reserve oil. In a bowl, lightly beat eggs. Mix in potatoes, onion and red pepper (capsicum) and chopped parsley. Season. Leave for 10 minutes. Wipe pan with absorbent kitchen paper. Add sufficient reserved oil to cover base in a thin film. Add egg mixture, spreading it evenly in pan. Cook over moderate heat, shaking pan occasion-ally, until underside is set and beginning to brown.

Cover pan with a large plate and hold in place with one hand. Quickly turn pan upside down so omelette falls onto plate. Return pan to heat, add a little more oil, then slide omelette into pan, cooked side uppermost (see Note opposite). Cook until lightly browned underneath. Slide onto a serving plate. Serve warm or at room temperature.

Serves 4 as a main course, or 8 as a tapa.

—LENTIL & CHORIZO POTAJE—

450 g (1 lb) green or brown lentils
1 Spanish onion, chopped
2 carrots, chopped
6 cloves garlic
175-225 g (6-8 oz) cooking chorizo
115 g (4 oz) piece belly pork, rind removed
1 bay leaf
2 beefsteak tomatoes, peeled, seeded and chopped
1 red pepper (capsicum), seeded and chopped
1 ½ tablespoons olive oil
1 Spanish onion, finely chopped
salt and freshly ground black pepper

Put lentils, chopped onion, carrots, garlic, chorizo, pork, bay leaf, tomatoes and pepper (capsicum) into a flameproof casserole or a saucepan. Just cover with water and bring to boil. Cover and simmer gently for about 30 minutes until lentils are tender, pork is cooked and there is sufficient liquid left to make a thick soup.

Meanwhile, heat oil in a heavy-based casserole, add finely chopped onion and cook very gently for about 15 minutes, stirring occasionally, until soft and lightly caramelised. Stir into lentils and season with salt and pepper. Discard bay leaf. Slice chorizo and pork and return to lentils and heat through.

Serves 4-5.

SPICY CHICK PEA POTAJE

225 g (8 oz) chick peas, soaked overnight, then drained
4 tablespoons olive oil
1 slice bread, crusts removed
1 Spanish onion, finely chopped
225 g (8 oz) cooking chorizo, thickly sliced
3 beefsteak tomatoes, peeled, seeded and chopped
1 tablespoon paprika
¼-½ teaspoon cumin seeds, finely crushed
450 g (1 lb) spinach, trimmed and chopped
3 cloves garlic

Cook chick peas in 1½ times their volume of boiling water for 1½-2 hours until tender.

Meanwhile, heat 2 tablespoons oil in a small frying pan, add bread and fry until golden on both sides. Remove and drain on absorbent kitchen paper. Add onion to pan and cook slowly, stirring occasionally, for 5 minutes. Add chorizo and cook for further 5-10 minutes until onion has softened but not coloured. Stir tomatoes into onion and cook, stirring occasionally, for about 10 minutes.

Heat remaining oil in a saucepan, stir in paprika and cumin, then add spinach. Cook until spinach has wilted. Using a pestle and mortar, pound garlic with a pinch of salt. Add fried bread and pound again. Drain chick peas, reserving liquid. Stir chick peas into spinach with tomato and garlic mixtures, and 175 ml (6 fl oz/¾ cup) chick pea liquid. Cover pan and simmer for about 30 minutes; add more liquid if mixture becomes too dry.

Serves 4.

— WHITE SOUP WITH GRAPES —

200 g (7 oz) shelled almonds
4 slices day-old, firm white bread, crusts removed,
    soaked in cold water and squeezed dry
3 cloves garlic, crushed
115 ml (4 fl oz/½ cup) olive oil
2-3 tablespoons sherry vinegar
salt
225 g (8 oz) muscat or other well-flavoured grapes,
    peeled and seeded, if necessary
chopped fresh parsley, to garnish

Place almonds in a bowl and pour over boiling water. Leave for 30 seconds, then remove nuts and squeeze them so the nuts pop out of their skins. Place nuts, bread and garlic in a food processor or blender and mix until smooth. With motor running, slowly pour in the oil. Add sufficient cold water, about 550 ml (20 fl oz/2½ cups), to give a creamy consistency.

Add vinegar and salt to taste. Add grapes and chill well. Pour into a cold soup tureen or individual soup bowls. Serve garnished with chopped parsley.

Serves 4-6.

GAZPACHO

750 g (1½ lb) beefsteak tomatoes
½ Spanish onion, chopped
1 green pepper (capsicum), chopped
1 red pepper (capsicum), chopped
2 cloves garlic, chopped
2 slices firm white bread, crusts removed, broken into
    pieces
300 ml (10 fl oz/1¼ cups) tomato juice
3 tablespoons virgin olive oil
2 tablespoons sherry vinegar
salt and freshly ground black pepper
about 8 ice cubes, to serve
ACCOMPANIMENTS:
1 diced small red pepper (capsicum), 1 diced small
    green pepper (capsicum), 1 diced small onion,
    1 chopped hard-boiled egg and croûtons

Peel, seed and chop tomatoes. Put in a food processor or blender with remaining soup ingredients, except ice cubes. Mix until smooth. Pour soup through a nylon sieve, pressing down well on contents of sieve. If necessary, thin soup with cold water, then chill well.

Place accompaniments in separate bowls. Adjust seasoning of soup, if necessary, then pour into cold soup bowls. Add ice cubes and serve with accompaniments.

Serves 4.

Variation: Do not sieve the soup if more texture is preferred.

—ROAST MONKFISH & GARLIC—

1 kg (2 lb) monkfish tail or two 450 g (1 lb) pieces,
  skinned
2 heads plump garlic, divided into cloves
2 tablespoons olive oil
salt and freshly ground black pepper
¼ teaspoon fresh thyme leaves
¼ teaspoon fennel seeds
juice 1 lemon
1 bay leaf
1 large red pepper (capsicum), peeled, seeded and cut
  into strips

Preheat oven to 220C (425F/Gas 7). Make
sure membrane has been removed from fish.
Cut out bone, then tie fish back into shape.

Using the point of a sharp knife, make some
incisions in fish. Cut 2 garlic cloves into thin
slices and push into incisions. Heat 1 tablespoon oil in a frying pan, add fish and brown
on all sides for about 5 minutes. Remove and
season with salt, pepper, thyme, fennel and
lemon juice.

Place fish on bay leaf in roasting tin. Arrange
remaining garlic around fish. Bake for 15
minutes. Add pepper (capsicum) strips and
cook for about 5 minutes until fish flakes
when pierced with a knife. Arrange fish,
garlic, pepper (capsicum) and cooking juices
on a plate. Carve fish in thin slices.

Serves 4.

— SOLE WITH GREEN DRESSING —

flour for coating
salt and freshly ground black pepper
1 egg, lightly beaten
about 100 g (3½ oz/1½ cups) fresh breadcrumbs
4 fillets sole or plaice, about 175 g (6 oz) each
4 tablespoons olive oil
lemon wedges and fresh herbs, to garnish
GREEN DRESSING:
3 cloves garlic
6 canned anchovy fillets, chopped
3 tablespoons finely chopped fresh parsley
½ teaspoon chopped fresh oregano
1½ tablespoons finely chopped capers
1½ tablespoons lemon juice
150 ml (5 fl oz/⅔ cup) virgin olive oil

To make the dressing, using a pestle and mortar, crush garlic with anchovies, then mix in parsley, oregano, capers and lemon juice. Beat in oil very slowly; set aside. Put flour on a plate and season with salt and pepper. Put egg and breadcrumbs on separate plates. Coat fish in seasoned flour, then dip in egg. Allow excess to drain off, then coat fish lightly and evenly in breadcrumbs. Set aside for 5 minutes.

Heat oil in a large frying pan, add fish and cook until golden and crisp and flesh flakes easily, about 3 minutes each side. Cook fish in batches if necessary so pan is not crowded. Using a fish slice, transfer fish to absorbent kitchen paper to drain. Garnish with lemon wedges and herbs. Stir dressing and serve with hot fish.

Serves 4.

MULLET WITH ANCHOVY SAUCE

4 red mullet, about 225 g (8 oz) each, scaled and
    cleaned
8 canned anchovy fillets, rinsed
flour for coating
salt and freshly ground black pepper
115 ml (4 fl oz/½ cup) freshly squeezed orange juice
4 tablespoons skinned, seeded and chopped tomato
chopped fresh parsley, capers and 1 orange, peeled and
    divided into segments, to garnish

Preheat grill. Using the point of a sharp
knife, cut 2 diagonal slashes in both sides of
each fish. Cut 4 anchovy fillets into 4 pieces
and insert one piece in each slash. Roughly
chop remaining anchovy fillets. Season flour
with salt and pepper, then coat fish lightly
and evenly.

Brush fish with oil, then place under very hot
grill until crisp and flesh flakes easily, about 5
minutes each side. Transfer to a warm serving
plate and keep warm. Stir orange juice,
tomato and chopped anchovies into juices
in grill pan, then pour into a saucepan, place
over direct heat and bubble until thickened
to a light sauce. Add pepper. Pour sauce
around fish and garnish with parsley, capers
and orange segments.

Serves 4.

-HAKE WITH PEAS & POTATOES-

½ Spanish onion, thinly sliced
8 cloves garlic, sliced
4 potatoes, thinly sliced
3 sprigs parsley
1 bay leaf
salt
4 hake steaks, about 225 g (8 oz) each
225 g (8 oz) shelled fresh peas, or frozen peas
6 tablespoons olive oil
1 tablespoon paprika

Put onion, 2 cloves garlic, the potatoes, parsley and bay leaf in a heavy flameproof casserole.

Just cover with cold water, add salt and simmer for 10 minutes. Add hake and fresh peas and simmer gently for about 10 minutes until vegetables are tender and fish flakes easily; if using frozen peas, add about 3 minutes before the end of cooking time. Strain off excess cooking liquid.

Meanwhile, in a small frying pan, heat oil, add remaining garlic and fry for 4-5 minutes until lightly coloured. Remove from heat and sprinkle in paprika. Stir quickly and pour over fish, potatoes and peas. Serve immediately.

Serves 4.

—COD WITH A PARSLEY CRUST—

750 g (1½ lb) cod, haddock or hake fillets, skinned
salt and freshly ground black pepper
2 cloves garlic, crushed
85 ml (3 fl oz/⅓ cup) olive oil
55 g (2 oz/1 cup) fresh breadcrumbs
2 tablespoons chopped fresh parsley
4 tablespoons lemon juice
parsley and lime wedges, to garnish

Season fish with salt and pepper and put in a shallow baking dish.

Mix together garlic and 4 tablespoons oil and pour over fish. Leave in a cool place for 1 hour. Preheat oven to 180C (350F/Gas 4).

Mix together breadcrumbs, parsley and lemon juice. Sprinkle evenly over fish, then trickle over remaining olive oil. Bake for about 15 minutes until fish flakes when tested with point of a sharp knife. Serve garnished with parsley and lime wedges.

Serves 4.

FISH IN GREEN SAUCE

3 tablespoons olive oil
4 hake or cod steaks, about 175 g (6 oz) each
½ Spanish onion, finely chopped
3 cloves garlic, chopped
115 ml (4 fl oz/½ cup) fish stock
2 tablespoons chopped fresh parsley
85 g (3 oz/¾ cup) slivered, roasted almonds
salt and freshly ground black pepper
dill sprigs, to garnish

Heat oil in a frying pan, add fish and cook for 2 minutes on each side.

Using a fish slice, transfer fish to a warmed plate, cover and keep warm. Add onion to oil remaining in pan and fry for 3 minutes. Stir in garlic and fry for 3 minutes, then stir in stock, parsley and almonds. Simmer for about 3 minutes until lightly thickened.

Transfer almond mixture to a blender or food processor and process until smooth. Season with salt and pepper. Return fish to pan, pour the sauce over the top and heat through for 1-2 minutes. Serve garnished with dill.

Serves 4.

ZARZUELA

16 mussels
350 g (12 oz) squid
3 tablespoons olive oil
450 g (1 lb) uncooked prawns in their shells
550 g (1¼ lb) monkfish, cut into 4 slices
salt and freshly ground black pepper
4 tablespoons Spanish brandy
1 large Spanish onion, finely chopped
1 teaspoon paprika
2 beefsteak tomatoes, peeled, seeded and chopped
1 bay leaf
115 ml (4 fl oz/½ cup) dry white wine
115 ml (4 fl oz/½ cup) fish stock
3 saffron threads, crushed
3 cloves garlic
3 tablespoons chopped fresh parsley

Clean and cook mussels (see page 12), remove from shells and set aside. Clean squid, chop tentacles and slice bodies into rings; set aside.

Heat 3 tablespoons oil in a large flameproof casserole. Add prawns and fry until pink. Transfer to a plate. Season monkfish, add to oil and fry over medium heat until light brown. Add squid rings and tentacles and fry briefly. Pour in brandy, then set brandy alight. When flames die down, tip contents of casserole into a bowl and set aside.

Add onion to casserole and cook gently for about 4 minutes until soft. Stir in paprika and cook for 30-60 seconds.

Stir tomatoes into casserole with bay leaf and simmer for 2-3 minutes. Stir in wine and boil until reduced by a third. Stir in stock and simmer for 3-4 minutes.

Pound saffron, garlic and parsley together, mix in a little hot stock, then return to casserole. Boil for 1 minute. Add contents of bowl, the mussels and prawns and cook gently for about 5 minutes.

Serves 4.

COD & AUBERGINE

1 aubergine (eggplant), cubed
salt and freshly ground black pepper
750 g (1½ lb) thick cod fillet, cut into 4
150 g (5 oz) cured chorizo, skinned and thinly sliced
4 tablespoons olive oil
1 Spanish onion, finely chopped
2 cloves garlic, very finely chopped
1 red pepper (capsicum), peeled, seeded and cut into strips
450 g (1 lb) beefsteak tomatoes, peeled, seeded and chopped
115 ml (4 fl oz/½ cup) dry white wine
chopped fresh parsley, to garnish

Place aubergine (eggplant) in a colander, sprinkle with salt and leave for 30 minutes. Rinse well and dry with absorbent kitchen paper. Halve each piece of cod horizontally without cutting completely in half. Open out like a book. Lay a quarter of the chorizo on one 'page' of each 'book', then cover with other 'page'. Heat oil in a flameproof casserole, add fish and cook until evenly browned. Using a fish slice, remove fish from casserole and set aside.

Add onion to casserole and cook slowly, for about 7 minutes, stirring occasionally, until soft but not coloured. Stir in garlic, aubergine (eggplant), and pepper (capsicum). Cook for about 4 minutes, then add tomatoes and wine and simmer for about 20 minutes until vegetables are tender. Season tomato mixture and return fish to casserole. Cook for a further 10 minutes. Garnish with parsley.

Serves 4.

CHICKEN WITH SHERRY

4 tablespoons raisins
225 ml (8 fl oz / 1 cup) oloroso sherry
3 tablespoons olive oil
1.75 kg (3½ lb) chicken, cut into 8 pieces (see page 66)
1 Spanish onion, finely chopped
1 clove garlic, finely chopped
225 ml (8 fl oz / 1 cup) chicken stock
salt and freshly ground black pepper
4 tablespoons pine nuts

In a small bowl, soak raisins in sherry for 30 minutes.

In a flameproof casserole, heat 2 tablespoons oil, add chicken and cook gently until lightly and evenly browned, about 10 minutes. Transfer to absorbent kitchen paper to drain. Add onion and garlic to casserole and cook gently, stirring occasionally, until softened and lightly coloured, about 7 minutes. Strain raisins and set aside.

Stir sherry into casserole. Simmer until reduced by half. Add stock, chicken and seasoning, bring to boil, then simmer gently until chicken is cooked, about 35 minutes. In a small pan, fry nuts in remaining oil until lightly coloured. Drain on absorbent kitchen paper, then stir into casserole with raisins. Transfer chicken to a warm serving dish. Boil liquid in casserole to concentrate slightly. Pour over chicken.

Serves 4.

SPICY CHICKEN

4 tablespoons olive oil
4 slices day-old French bread
8 cloves garlic
1.75 kg (3½ lb) chicken, skinned and cut into small
   pieces
300 ml (10 fl oz/1¼ cups) medium-bodied dry white
   wine
large pinch saffron threads, finely crushed
3 tablespoons chopped fresh parsley
3 cloves
freshly grated nutmeg
salt and freshly ground black pepper

Heat oil in a flameproof casserole, add bread and 5 garlic cloves and fry until browned.

Transfer to a mortar and crush, then transfer to a bowl. Crush remaining garlic and add to casserole with chicken. Cook until chicken changes colour. Pour in wine and just enough water to cover chicken. Cover casserole and simmer gently for about 30 minutes until chicken juices run clear when thickest part is pierced with a sharp knife.

Meanwhile, in a bowl dissolve saffron in 2 tablespoons of the chicken cooking liquid. Put parsley, cloves and nutmeg in the mortar and pound to a paste. Stir in the saffron. Mix with crushed bread, then stir the mixture into the casserole and cook for 10 minutes. Season to taste and serve.

Serves 4.

CHICKEN PEPITORIA

2 tablespoons olive oil
1.75 kg (3½ lb) chicken, cut into 8 pieces, or 4 large
   chicken portions, halved
½ Spanish onion, finely chopped
115 g (4 oz) serrano ham, cut into strips
225 ml (8 fl oz/1 cup) chicken stock
4 cloves garlic, crushed
20 g (¾ oz/15) almonds or hazelnuts, lightly roasted
pinch ground cloves
3 tablespoons chopped fresh parsley
3 egg yolks
salt and freshly ground black pepper

Heat oil in a flameproof casserole, add chicken and fry until lightly browned all over. Using a slotted spoon, remove chicken from casserole and set aside. Add onion to casserole and cook for about 4 minutes, stirring occasionally. Stir in ham, cook for 1 minute, then return chicken to casserole. Pour in the stock, cover tightly and simmer gently for about 45 minutes until chicken is tender.

Meanwhile, pound together garlic, nuts, cloves and parsley. Place in a small bowl and gradually work in egg yolks. Stir a little hot chicken liquid into the bowl, then stir mixture into the casserole. Continue to cook gently, stirring, until sauce thickens; do not allow to boil. Season with salt and pepper.

Serves 4.

CHICKEN & ALLIOLI

4 chicken portions
salt and freshly ground black pepper
6 tablespoons olive oil
3 tablespoons lemon juice
2 tablespoons finely chopped spring onions
2 tablespoons chopped fresh parsley
Allioli, see page 24
2 lemons, quartered

Rub chicken with salt and pepper, then place in a single layer in a non-metallic dish.

Pour the oil and lemon juice over the chicken and leave for 1 hour, turning chicken over once or twice.

Preheat grill. Place chicken on a grill rack and grill slowly for 8-10 minutes on each side, basting occasionally with the oil and lemon mixture, until crisp on the outside and tender throughout. Transfer to a warm serving plate and scatter spring onions and parsley over the top. Serve with Allioli and lemon quarters.

Serves 4.

QUAIL WITH GRAPES

3 tablespoons olive oil
1 Spanish onion, finely chopped
2 small carrots, finely chopped
salt and freshly ground black pepper
8 quail
8 slices streaky bacon
4 black peppercorns
2 cloves garlic
250 g (9 oz) moscatel grapes, peeled and seeded
pinch freshly grated nutmeg
225 ml (8 fl oz/1 cup) medium-bodied dry white wine
4 tablespoons Spanish brandy

Preheat oven to 190C (375F/Gas 5). Heat oil in a heavy flameproof casserole that will hold the quail in a single layer. Add onion and carrots and cook, stirring occasionally, for 4-5 minutes. Season quail inside and out, lay a slice of bacon over each one and tie in place with string. Place on the vegetables, then cook in the oven for 30 minutes.

Meanwhile, using a pestle and mortar, crush peppercorns and garlic, then work in half the grapes, the nutmeg, wine and brandy. Pour the mixture over the quail and cook for 30 minutes, basting occasionally. Add remaining grapes, then carefully pour cooking liquid into a saucepan; keep casserole warm. Boil liquid until lightly thickened, then season to taste. Transfer quail, bacon, vegetables and grapes to a warm serving plate and pour the sauce over them.

Serves 4-6.

SPANISH PARTRIDGE

2 partridges, halved along backbone
2 tablespoons brandy
salt and freshly ground black pepper
3 tablespoons olive oil
1 Spanish onion, chopped
3 cloves garlic, finely chopped
2 tablespoons plain flour
4 tablespoons red wine vinegar
225 ml (8 fl oz/1 cup) red wine
225 ml (8 fl oz/1 cup) chicken stock
6 black peppercorns
2 cloves
1 bay leaf
2 carrots, cut into short lengths
8 shallots
25 g (1 oz) plain (dark) chocolate, grated

Rub partridges with brandy, salt and pepper and set aside for 30 minutes. Heat oil in a heavy flameproof casserole into which the birds fit snugly. Add onion and fry, stirring occasionally, for 3 minutes. Stir in garlic and cook for 2 minutes.

Sprinkle birds lightly with flour, then fry in casserole for 5 minutes each side. Remove and set aside.

Stir vinegar into casserole and boil for 1-2 minutes. Add wine and boil for 1-2 minutes, then add stock, peppercorns, cloves, bay leaf and partridges. Heat to simmering point, cover tightly and cook gently for 40 minutes. Add carrots and shallots, cover again, and continue to cook gently for 20 minutes.

Transfer partridges, shallots and carrots to a warm dish. If necessary, boil the cooking juices until reduced to 300 ml (10 fl oz/ 1¼ cups), then purée in a blender or food processor.

Return juices to casserole, heat gently and stir in chocolate until melted. Return partridges and vegetables to casserole and turn them over in the sauce so they are well coated.

Serves 4.

DUCK & OLIVES

3 tablespoons olive oil
2-2.5 kg (4-5 lb) duck, cut into 4 pieces
1 Spanish onion, finely chopped
1 tablespoon plain flour
2 beefsteak tomatoes, peeled, seeded and chopped
175 ml (6 fl oz/¾ cup) dry white wine
3 tablespoons water
4 bay leaves
3 sprigs parsley
3 cloves garlic, crushed
salt and freshly ground black pepper
225 g (8 oz) green olives

Heat half the oil in a heavy flameproof casserole. Add duck in batches, brown evenly, then transfer to absorbent kitchen paper to drain. Heat remaining oil in casserole, add onion and cook for 6-8 minutes, stirring occasionally, until golden and translucent. Stir in flour, then tomatoes, wine, water, bay leaves, parsley and garlic. Season with salt and pepper. Bring to boil, stirring. Add duck pieces, cover and cook gently for 30 minutes.

Put olives into a bowl, pour over boiling water, then drain well. Add to casserole, cover tightly and cook for about 30 minutes until juices run clear when thickest part of duck is pierced with a skewer. Skim excess fat from surface, and adjust seasoning, if necessary.

Serves 4.

LAMB CHILINDRON

4 tablespoons olive oil
750 g (1½ lb) lean lamb, cubed
salt and freshly ground black pepper
1 Spanish onion, chopped
2 cloves garlic, chopped
3 large red peppers (capsicums), peeled, seeded and
  cut into strips
4 beefsteak tomatoes, peeled, seeded and chopped
1 dried red chilli, chopped
chopped fresh herbs, to garnish

Heat oil in a flameproof casserole. Season
lamb and add to casserole.

Cook, stirring, until evenly browned, then
using a slotted spoon, transfer to a bowl. Add
onion to casserole and cook for about 4
minutes, stirring occasionally, until softened
but not coloured. Stir in garlic, cook for 1-2
minutes, then stir in peppers (capsicums),
tomatoes and chilli. Simmer for 5 minutes.

Return lamb, and any juices that have
collected in bowl, to casserole. Cover tightly
and cook gently for about 1½ hours until
lamb is tender. Season if necessary. Serve
garnished with chopped herbs.

Serves 6.

—LAMB WITH BLACK OLIVES—

4 tablespoons olive oil
750 g (1½ lb) lean lamb, cut into small cubes
115 g (4 oz) piece belly pork, cut into small strips
2 cloves garlic, sliced
½-1 teaspoon chopped fresh oregano
175 ml (6 fl oz/¾ cup) full-bodied white wine
1 fresh red chilli, seeded and finely chopped
12-15 black olives, stoned

Heat oil in a wide, shallow flameproof casserole. Add lamb, pork and garlic and cook over a high heat to seal and brown meat.

In a small saucepan, boil oregano and wine for 2-3 minutes. Stir into casserole, cover and cook gently for 30 minutes.

Stir chilli and olives into casserole. Cover again and cook for about 30 minutes until lamb is tender. If necessary, uncover casserole towards end of cooking time so liquid can evaporate to make a light sauce.

Serves 4.

–LAMB WITH LEMON & GARLIC–

3 tablespoons olive oil
1 kg (2¼ lb) lean, boneless lamb, cut into 2.5 cm (1 in)
   pieces
1 Spanish onion, finely chopped
3 cloves garlic, crushed
1 tablespoon paprika
3 tablespoons finely chopped fresh parsley
3 tablespoons lemon juice
salt and freshly ground black pepper
3 tablespoons dry white wine (optional)

Heat oil in a heavy flameproof casserole, add lamb and cook, stirring occasionally, until lightly browned. Do this in batches if necessary so the pieces are not crowded. Using a slotted spoon, transfer meat to a plate or bowl and reserve.

Stir onion into casserole and cook for about 5 minutes, stirring occasionally, until softened. Stir in garlic, cook for 2 minutes, then stir in paprika. When well blended, stir in lamb and any juices on plate or in bowl, the parsley, lemon juice and seasoning. Cover tightly and cook over very low heat for 1¼-1½ hours, shaking casserole occasionally, until lamb is very tender. If necessary, add wine or 3 tablespoons water.

Serves 4-6.

– BRAISED LAMB & VEGETABLES –

450 g (1 lb) firm, yellow-flesh potatoes, cut into 0.5 cm
  (¼ in) slices
2 cloves garlic, pounded to a paste
6-8 spring onions, thinly sliced
2 medium-large artichoke bottoms (see page 50), sliced
150 g (5 oz) chestnut mushrooms, chopped
handful parsley, finely chopped
1 tablespoon mixed herbs, chopped
salt and freshly ground black pepper
3 tablespoons olive oil
4 lamb shoulder or loin chops
175 ml (6 fl oz/¾ cup) full-bodied dry white wine

Preheat oven to 190C (375F/Gas 5). In a
bowl, combine potatoes, garlic, spring
onions, artichoke bottoms, mushrooms,
parsley, mixed herbs and seasoning. Place
half the mixture in a heavy flameproof
casserole. Heat oil in a frying pan, add lamb
and brown on both sides. Drain on absorbent
kitchen paper, then season and place in
casserole.

Over the heat, stir wine into pan to dislodge
cooking juices, bring to boil and pour over
lamb. Cover with remaining vegetables and
add sufficient water to come almost to the
level of the vegetables. Bring to the boil,
cover and cook in the oven for about 30
minutes. Uncover and cook for a further 1
hour. Add a little water if it seems to be
drying out.

Serves 4.

SPICED PORK LOIN

1 tablespoon paprika
3 cloves garlic, finely crushed
1 teaspoon chopped fresh oregano
½ teaspoon finely crushed cumin seeds
1 bay leaf, crushed
salt
3 tablespoons virgin olive oil
750 g (1½ lb) boned and rolled loin of pork
olive oil for frying
4 tablespoons full-bodied dry white wine
stoned green olives, to serve

In a small bowl, mix together paprika, garlic, oregano, cumin seeds, bay leaf and salt, then stir in olive oil.

Place pork in a non-metallic dish, spoon the marinade mixture over the top, cover and leave in refrigerator for 2-3 days. Return pork to room temperature 30 minutes before cooking.

Cut pork into 4 slices. Heat oil in a frying pan over fairly high heat. Add pork, brown quickly on both sides, then cook more gently for 4-5 minutes a side until cooked through. Transfer slices to a warm serving plate. Stir wine into cooking juices, boil for 2-3 minutes, then pour over pork. Scatter green olives over the top.

Serves 4.

—BEEF WITH TOMATO SAUCE—

2 cloves garlic, thinly sliced
1 tablespoon finely chopped fresh thyme
1 tablespoon finely chopped fresh marjoram
750 g (1½ lb) piece chuck steak
2 tablespoons olive oil
SAUCE:
2 tablespoons olive oil
8 cloves garlic, chopped
1 sprig thyme
2 sprigs marjoram
3 sprigs parsley
400 g (14 oz) can chopped tomatoes
8 canned anchovy fillets, chopped
175 ml (6 fl oz/¾ cup) dry white wine
24 small black olives, stoned
salt and freshly ground black pepper

To make the sauce, heat oil in a saucepan, add garlic and herbs and cook gently for 5 minutes. Add tomatoes with their juice, then stir in anchovies, wine and olives. Simmer for 15 minutes. Taste and adjust seasoning.

Meanwhile, mix sliced garlic with chopped herbs. Using the point of a sharp knife, cut small slits in beef and push the herb-covered slices of garlic deep into slits. Heat oil in a flameproof casserole, add beef and cook until evenly browned, 10 minutes. Pour over sauce, cover tightly and cook gently for about 1½ hours turning beef occasionally, until it is tender.

Serves 4.

GARLIC BEEF

2 tablespoons olive oil
115 g (4 oz) piece green (unsmoked) bacon, cut into
   5 cm (2 in) cubes
1 kg (2 lb) chuck steak, cut into 4 cm (1½ in) cubes
1 Spanish onion, chopped
1 head garlic, divide into cloves
225 ml (8 fl oz/1 cup) red wine
2 cloves
bouquet garni of 1 sprig marjoram, 1 sprig thyme, 2
   sprigs parsley and 1 bay leaf
salt and freshly ground black pepper

In a heavy flameproof casserole, heat oil, add
bacon and cook over a low heat until bacon
gives off its fat. Increase heat, add beef and
cook for about 5 minutes, stirring occasionally, until browned all over. Using a slotted
spoon, transfer beef and bacon to a bowl.

Stir onion and garlic into casserole and cook
gently for 6 minutes, stirring occasionally.
Stir in wine, cloves, bouquet garni and salt
and pepper. Return meat to casserole, cover
tightly and cook gently for 2 hours, stirring
occasionally, until meat is very tender.
Check from time to time to ensure casserole is
not drying out.

Serves 6.

RICE & BLACK BEANS

2 tablespoons olive oil
1 Spanish onion, chopped
2 cloves garlic, chopped
115 g (4 oz) bacon, chopped
1 small red pepper (capsicum), chopped
1 teaspoon paprika
300 g (10 oz) beefsteak tomatoes, peeled, seeded and
    chopped
salt and freshly ground black pepper
225 g (8 oz) risotto rice
herb sprigs, to garnish
BEANS:
225 g (8 oz) black beans, soaked overnight and drained
½ Spanish onion
2 cloves garlic, crushed

To prepare the beans, put them in a saucepan with onion and garlic. Cover with plenty of water, bring to the boil, then simmer for 1½-2 hours until just tender. Meanwhile, in a saucepan, heat oil, add chopped onion, garlic, bacon and red pepper (capsicum) and cook, stirring occasionally, until bacon begins to brown. Stir in paprika for 30-60 seconds, then stir in tomatoes and cook for about 5 minutes, stirring occasionally. Season well.

Stir rice and 450 ml (16 fl oz/2 cups) water into pan with tomato mixture. Bring to the boil, stir, then simmer gently for about 25 minutes until liquid is absorbed and rice tender. Drain beans. Discard onion and garlic. Stir the beans into the rice mixture. Adjust seasoning and serve garnished with sprigs of herbs.

Serves 4-6.

Please disregard page reference to Allioli on page 8.
Please disregard page references in ingredients on pages 43 and 54.

PAELLA

4 tablespoons olive oil
1 kg (2 lb) chicken, cut into small pieces
2 Spanish onions, chopped
4 cloves garlic, chopped
1 tablespoon paprika
350 g (12 oz) risotto rice
3 beefsteak tomatoes, peeled, seeded and chopped
1.75 litres (3 pints/7½ cups) boiling chicken stock
1 sprig rosemary
salt and freshly ground black pepper
large pinch saffron threads, finely crushed
225 g (8 oz) small squid
150 g (5 oz) green beans
450 g (1 lb) mussels in their shells
225 g (8 oz) raw prawns in their shells
115 g (4 oz) broad beans

Heat oil in a 40 cm (16 in) paella or 4 litre (7 pint/18 cup) wide shallow casserole pan. Add chicken and cook for about 10 minutes until lightly browned. Add onions and garlic and fry for 5 minutes, then stir in paprika followed by rice. Stir for 2-3 minutes. Stir tomatoes into paella with stock, rosemary and salt and pepper. Dissolve saffron in 2 tablespoons stock, then add to paella. Boil for 8-10 minutes.

Prepare squid, see page 17; cut bodies into rings and chop tentacles. Cut green beans into short lengths. Scatter all seafood, green beans and broad beans into paella – do not stir. Gradually turn down heat and simmer for 8-10 minutes until rice is tender and liquid absorbed. Cover, remove from heat and leave for 5-10 minutes.

Serves 4.

Variation: Add 4 small rabbit portions with the chicken pieces.

SPICED RICE & PEPPERS

4 tablespoons olive oil
225 g (8 oz) long-grain rice
2 cloves garlic
salt
1 teaspoon each cumin and coriander seeds
3 tablespoons tomato purée (paste)
2 teaspoons paprika
1 teaspoon chilli powder
pinch saffron threads, crushed and dissolved in 2
    tablespoons boiling water
550 ml (20 fl oz/2½ cups) boiling chicken or vegetable
    stock or water
3-4 red peppers (capsicums), peeled, halved lengthways
    and seeded
extra virgin olive oil, to serve (optional)
chopped fresh herbs, to garnish

Heat oil in a paella pan or wide, heavy-based shallow saucepan. Stir in rice, then stir-fry for 2-3 minutes. Meanwhile, using a pestle and mortar, grind together garlic, salt, cumin and coriander seeds, then stir in tomato purée (paste), paprika, chilli and saffron liquid. Stir into rice. Stir in stock or water. Bring to boil, then cover and simmer for about 7 minutes.

Arrange peppers (capsicums) around sides of pan. Simmer for 7-10 minutes until rice is tender and plump, and liquid absorbed. Remove from heat and leave for 5 minutes. Trickle extra virgin oil over peppers (capsicums), if desired, and garnish with chopped herbs.

Serves 4.

ASPARAGUS WITH EGG

750 g (1½ lb) fresh asparagus
1 hard-boiled egg, finely chopped
85 ml (3 fl oz/⅓ cup) olive oil
1 clove garlic
45 g (1½ oz/¾ cup) fresh, coarse breadcrumbs
2 tablespoons chopped fresh parsley

Using a small sharp knife, cut off woody part at end of asparagus stems. Working from tip to base, scrape off scales from stems.

Tie stems into 4 bundles with tape or string. Bring 5 cm (2 in) level of water to the boil in a deep saucepan, add asparagus bundles, tips pointing upwards. Cover pan with a lid or dome of foil and simmer for 8-10 minutes until asparagus is just tender. Remove asparagus and untie bundles. Drain asparagus on a thick pad of absorbent kitchen paper. Arrange on a warm serving plate, sprinkle egg over stems, cover and keep warm.

Meanwhile, heat oil in a frying pan, add garlic and fry until lightly browned. Discard garlic. Stir breadcrumbs into pan and cook for 5-7 minutes, stirring, until crisp and golden. Remove from heat, stir in parsley, then pour it over the asparagus, leaving tips uncovered. Serve immediately.

Serves 4.

PISTO MANCHEGO

2 tablespoons olive oil
55 g (2 oz) bacon, chopped
2 large Spanish onions, chopped
1 clove garlic, chopped
2 courgettes (zucchini), chopped
4 red peppers (capsicums), peeled and chopped
450 g (1 lb) beefsteak tomatoes, peeled, seeded and
   chopped
bunch mint, parsley and basil, chopped
salt and freshly ground black pepper
4 poached or fried eggs, to serve (optional)

In a large frying pan, heat oil, add bacon, onions and garlic and cook gently for about 15 minutes, stirring occasionally, until onions are very soft and lightly coloured.

Add courgettes (zucchini) and peppers (capsicums) to pan and fry for about 4 minutes until soft. Stir in tomatoes and herbs and cook for 20-30 minutes until thickened. Season to taste. Serve topped by poached or fried eggs, if desired.

Serves 4.

—— SPINACH WITH RAISINS ——

50 g (2 oz) raisins
1 kg (2 lb) spinach
3 tablespoons olive oil
1 clove garlic, finely chopped
3 tablespoons pine nuts
salt and freshly ground black pepper
croûtons, to serve

Put raisins into a small bowl, cover with boiling water and leave to soak.

Wash spinach, shake off surplus water but do not dry the leaves. Put into a large saucepan, cover and cook until spinach wilts. Uncover and cook until excess moisture has evaporated. Chop coarsely. Drain raisins.

Heat oil in a frying pan, add garlic and pine nuts and fry, stirring occasionally, until beginning to colour. Stir in spinach and raisins, add salt and pepper and cook over low heat for 5 minutes. Serve with croûtons sprinkled over the top.

Serves 4.

— BAKED MIXED VEGETABLES —

450 g (1 lb) aubergines (eggplants), thinly sliced
salt and freshly ground black pepper
150 ml (5 fl oz/⅔ cup) olive oil
3 cloves garlic, crushed
450 g (1 lb) beefsteak tomatoes, peeled, seeded and
    chopped
1 tablespoon tomato purée (paste)
2 Spanish onions, thinly sliced
1 green pepper (capsicum), sliced
1 red pepper (capsicum), sliced
450 g (1 lb) potatoes, boiled and sliced
25 g (1 oz/½ cup) fresh breadcrumbs

Sprinkle aubergine (eggplant) slices with salt
and leave in a colander for 30 minutes. Rinse
under cold running water and dry well on
absorbent kitchen paper. Meanwhile, in a
saucepan, heat 1 tablespoon oil, add garlic
and fry gently without browning. Add
tomatoes, tomato purée (paste) and salt and
pepper. Cover and simmer for 15 minutes.
Preheat oven to 200C (400F/Gas 6). In a
frying pan, heat 4 tablespoons oil.

Add onions and peppers (capsicums); cook
gently for 15 minutes. Using a slotted spoon,
remove from pan; set aside. Add remaining
oil to pan. Add aubergine (eggplant) slices in
batches; fry until golden. Drain on absorbent
kitchen paper. Layer all the vegetables in a
baking dish; season each layer and moisten
with the tomato sauce. Finish with tomato
sauce. Sprinkle with breadcrumbs. Bake for
about 20 minutes until golden.

Serves 4-6.

—— BROAD BEANS WITH HAM ——

2 tablespoons olive oil
4 large spring onions, finely chopped
1 red pepper (capsicum), diced
55 g (2 oz) serrano ham, diced
450 g (1 lb) shelled broad beans
about 175 ml (6 fl oz/¾ cup) dry white wine
salt and freshly ground black pepper
chopped fresh herbs, to garnish (optional)

In a saucepan, heat oil, add spring onions,
pepper (capsicum) and ham and cook for 3
minutes.

Stir in beans and cook for 1 minute. Add
sufficient wine to cover, bring to boil, then
cover pan and simmer gently for about 20
minutes until beans are tender.

Uncover and boil off excess liquid. Add black
pepper, and salt, if necessary. Cool slightly
before serving. Garnish with chopped herbs,
if desired.

Serves 4.

CHURROS

olive oil for deep frying
mixture of vanilla caster sugar and icing sugar for
  dusting
DOUGH:
100 g (3½ oz/scant 1 cup) self-raising flour
¼ teaspoon ground cinnamon
55 g (2 oz/¼ cup) butter, diced
3-4 eggs, beaten

To make dough, sift flour and cinnamon onto
a plate, or into a bowl, and place beside hob.

Gently heat butter in 175 ml (6 fl oz/¾ cup)
water until butter has melted, then bring
quickly to boil. Immediately remove from
heat and quickly add flour mixture in one go
and beat vigorously until smooth. Return to
heat for about 30 seconds, still beating.
Remove from heat and allow to cool slightly.
Gradually beat in eggs until mixture is a
smooth, thick glossy paste. Half fill a deep fat
fryer or pan with oil and heat to 190C (375F).

Spoon dough into a piping bag fitted with a
0.5-1 cm (¼-½ in) plain nozzle and pipe 3 or
4 lengths into the hot oil, forming them into
rings, spirals or horseshoes; use a sharp knife
to cut off mixture at required length. Fry for
about 3 minutes, turning once, until golden.
Using a slotted spoon, transfer to absorbent
kitchen paper to drain. Keep warm while
frying remaining mixture. Dust thickly with
sugar mixture and serve hot.

Serves 4.

——OLIVE OIL & APPLE CAKE——

250 g (9 oz/2 cups plus 2 tablespoons) self-raising flour
¾ teaspoon ground cinnamon
85 g (3 oz/⅓ cup) caster sugar
finely grated rind and juice 1 lemon
2 eggs, beaten
3 tablespoons sweet sherry
160 ml (5½ fl oz/⅔ cup) olive oil
450 g (1 lb) crisp apples

Preheat oven to 180C (350F/Gas 4). Grease
an 18 cm (7 in) cake tin. In a bowl, stir
together flour, cinnamon, sugar and lemon
rind. Make a well in centre and gradually add
eggs, sherry, olive oil and lemon juice,
stirring to make a smooth mixture.

Peel, core and chop apples. Fold into cake
mixture and turn into prepared tin. Bake for
40-45 minutes until golden brown and firm to
the touch in centre. Leave for a few minutes
before turning onto a wire rack to cool.

Makes 8 slices.

LECHE FRITA

about 3 tablespoons caster sugar
3 eggs
55 g (2 oz/¹/₂ cup) plain flour
225 ml (8 fl oz/1 cup) whipping cream
225 ml (8 fl oz/1 cup) milk
few drops vanilla essence
100 g (3¹/₂ oz/1 cup) cake crumbs, preferably lemon
vegetable oil for deep frying

Lightly flour a baking sheet. In a bowl, beat together sugar and 2 eggs until pale. Gradually stir in flour.

In a heavy, preferably non-stick, saucepan, heat cream, milk and vanilla essence to boiling point. Slowly pour into the bowl, stirring. Return to heat and cook gently, stirring, until thickened; do not allow to boil. Pour onto baking sheet to make an even layer about 1 cm (¹/₂ in) thick, then leave to cool. Cover and refrigerate for at least 1 hour. Cut cold custard mixture into approximately 2.5 cm (1 in) squares rectangles or diamonds.

Beat remaining egg, then dip shapes first in beaten egg, then in the crumbs. Half fill a deep fat fryer or pan with vegetable oil and heat to 190C (375F). Add coated shapes in batches and cook for about 1¹/₂ minutes until golden and crisp on outside; keep an eye on temperature of the oil to make sure that it does not drop as the cubes should cook very quickly. Using a slotted spoon, transfer to absorbent kitchen paper, drain quickly and serve immediately.

Serves 4-6.

BUNUELOS

Churros dough, see page 108, made with 25 g (1 oz/6
  teaspoons) each butter and sugar, 5 tablespoons each
  milk and water, 55 g (2 oz/½ cup) self-raising flour,
  grated rind 1 lemon, 2½ eggs and 1 tablespoon
  Spanish brandy
olive oil for deep frying
2 tablespoons icing sugar
1 teaspoon ground cinnamon
FILLING:
85 g (3 oz/⅓ cup) caster sugar
85 g (3 oz/¾ cup) plain flour
2 eggs, beaten
500 ml (18 fl oz/2¼ cups) milk
grated rind 1 lemon
40 g (1½ oz/9 teaspoons) butter

To make filling, in a bowl, stir together sugar,
flour, eggs and a little milk. In a heavy,
preferably non-stick, saucepan, heat lemon
rind and remaining milk to boil. Slowly pour
into bowl, stirring. Return to pan. Heat
gently, stirring with a wooden spoon, until
sauce thickens; continue to heat gently for 5
minutes; do not allow to boil. Remove from
heat, stir in butter and cover closely with
greaseproof paper. Leave to cool.

Prepare dough, see page 108. Heat butter and
sugar in milk and water until butter has melted
and sugar dissolved. Add flour and lemon
rind, then beat in eggs and brandy. Heat oil in
a deep fat fryer to 180C (350F). Form dough
into small walnut-size balls and fry in batches
until evenly browned. Transfer to absorbent
kitchen paper while frying remaining mixture. Pierce a hole in the side of each ball and
fill with the filling. Serve hot dusted thickly
with the sugar mixed with the cinnamon.

Serves 4.

INDEX